The Big Book of
Fathers' Wit and Wisdom

First published in 2007 by
PRION
an imprint of the
Carlton Publishing Group
20 Mortimer Street
London W1T 3JW

Some of the material in this book was previously published by Prion in 2005 in *Fathers' Wit*.

A catalogue record for this book is available from the British Library.

ISBN 978 1 85375 639 9

Typeset by E–Type, Liverpool

Printed in Dubai

The Big Book of
Fathers' Wit and Wisdom

Humorous Quotes
on Being a Dad

Compiled by Rosemarie Jarski

Contents

Introduction

What has been proven to reduce crime, child poverty, mental illness, substance abuse, teenage pregnancy *and* requires no new taxes? The answer is Fatherhood. This being so, why is it that, with the exception of one-parent families and the elderly, there is no more beleaguered class in society today than fathers? Fathers are second-class citizens, sidelined, marginalized, ridiculed, castigated and undervalued. Listen to the news, pick up any newspaper, and you'd think there were only three kinds of dads: deadbeat, child abusers and deranged lunatics who dress up as superheroes and scale high buildings.

The Cult of Motherhood continues to flourish, but where are the worshippers at the Shrine of Fatherhood? Where is the biker with 'DAD' tattooed on his bicep? Where is the banner emblazoned with the slogan, 'Hello Dad'? When it comes to raising children, even the language is predicated against dads. 'Mothering' is defined as 'creating, nurturing and protecting'; 'Fathering' is defined as 'to procreate'. No emotional bond is implied.

Fathers have the Mother of all Battles getting the recognition they deserve. The only time affection and gratitude are sanctioned is on Father's Day. Did you know that there are more reverse-charge calls on Father's Day than on any other day of the year? So, it has come to this: children are now charging their dad to tell him they love him.

No man can give birth to a child, but no woman can give a father's love. This treasury of fathers' wit is a Valentine to Dad, a celebration of the unique and vital role he plays in shaping our lives. Papa is a man of many parts — protector, provider, playmate and, in the case of most daughters, pushover. Every stage of fatherhood is explored, from family planning to empty nest, tackling the issues that *really* preoccupy fathers — such as sex, nappy-changing, sex, the family car, sex, how to stop your teenage daughters having sex and sex. Daughters, sons, wives and other family members offer sharp observations but, quite properly, most of the voices belong to fathers themselves. Old or new, good or bad, present or absent, Dad is here in his infinite variety. The only criterion for inclusion is that he should have some gem of wit to impart.

Some of the best and funniest insights come from TV dads. President George Bush *Père* famously declared that families would do better to follow the example of the Waltons than the Simpsons. Which father would you prefer? John Walton is the perfect paterfamilias, promoting virtues of thrift and self-improvement, dispensing homespun wisdom and never failing to say goodnight to his children. Homer Simpson is an overweight, workshy slob who forgets to pick up his son, Bart, from soccer practice and gets mad when someone spanks him as his own preferred form of corporal punishment is strangulation; he refuses to take his daughter to a bookfair ('If it doesn't have Siamese twins in a jar, it's not a fair'), and when asked if he likes his kids, says, 'What do you mean, *all* the time? Even when they're *nuts*?'

The American public gave their answer by voting Homer Simpson 'Best TV Dad' in an online poll. How did he beat John Walton, who could only scrape ninth

place? *The Simpsons* offers a rounded view of average family life, showing that, while it can be wonderful, caring and fun, it can also be horrible, selfish and cruel. What lies at its heart, though, is love. 'Love,' said Peter Ustinov, 'is an act of endless forgiveness, a tender look which becomes a habit.' In families, forgiveness is in daily demand, and particularly so in father–son relationships. The parable of the Prodigal Son never goes out of fashion. Ernest Hemingway wrote a poignant short story called 'The Capital of the World' about a Spanish father who becomes estranged from his son. After an argument, the son leaves home and goes to Madrid. Years later, the father is desperate for a reconciliation and travels to Madrid. But he is unable to trace his son. More in hope than expectation, he places an ad in the local newspaper: 'Dear Paco. All is forgiven. Meet me Tuesday at noon in front of the Hotel Montana. Papa.' The father arrives in the square at the appointed time, and finds 800 young men named Paco all hoping to be reunited with their fathers.

So what's the secret of being a good dad

– apart from the obvious but critical, 'Know when to stop tickling'? The simple answer seeps through these pages by osmosis … Be There. To be in your child's memories tomorrow you have to be in their lives today. Not just for the so-called milestones like birthdays, concerts and graduations, but for those seemingly small everyday moments such as pushing a swing, sharing a pizza, reading a bedtime story. After all, you never know when you're making a memory. Boswell, the biographer of Samuel Johnson, would often refer to a day in his youth when his father took him fishing. He remembered the trip as a special time when his father taught him many lessons he carried with him through life. And how did Boswell's father remember the same excursion? The entry in his journal for that day records just a single sentence: 'Gone fishing today with my son; a day wasted.'

What Is a Father?

Directly after God in heaven comes Papa.

Wolfgang Amadeus Mozart

A father is a cash-point machine in trousers.

Martin Hart

A father is a man who carries photographs where his money used to be.

Anon

Daddies are for catching spiders.

Molly, **aged 4**

Father is the guy who's quick to appear with the camera and just as quick to disappear when there's a diaper to be changed.

Joan Rivers

A father is a man who prefers sleep over sex.

Ralph Anderson

A father is something mythical and infinitely important: a protector, who keeps a lid on all the chaotic and catastrophic possibilities of life.

Tom Wolfe

Any man can be a father. It takes someone special to be a dad.

Anon

The thing to remember about fathers is, they're men. A girl has to keep it in mind: they are dragon-seekers, bent on improbable rescues. Scratch any father, you find someone chock-full of qualms and romantic terrors, believing change is a threat – like your first shoes with heels on, like your first bicycle it took such months to get.

Phyllis McGinley

Fatherhood

What's it called when you're damned if you do, and damned if you don't? Oh, yes, fatherhood.
Paul Hennessy, 8 Simple Rules for Dating My Teenage Daughter

Fatherhood is pretending the present you love most is soap-on-a-rope.

Bill Cosby

Being a father is like doing drugs – you smell bad, get no sleep and spend all your money on them.

Paul Bettany

After all, I'm your father. It's true if it hadn't been me it would have been someone else. But that's no excuse.

Samuel Beckett

I make it a rule to pat all children on the head as I pass by – in case it is one of mine.

Augustus John

My dream would be to build a 2,000-foot statue of Homer Simpson with a revolving head and a restaurant inside it. A monument to fatherhood.

Matt Groening, creator of The Simpsons

To Breed or Not to Breed?

FAMILY PLANNING

You need a licence to buy a dog, to drive a car – hell, you need a licence to catch a fish. But they'll let any jackass be a father.

Martin Abbott

Parents are the very last people who ought to be allowed to have children.

Samuel Butler

Having a child is surely the most beautifully irrational act that two people in love can commit.

Bill Cosby

How could Tristan and Isolde, or Romeo and Juliet, have survived if there had been a child? All the poetry would have been lost in irritation at feeding time.

Peter Ustinov

My father had children because they were a by-product of sex.

Carrie Fisher

Familiarity breeds contempt – and children.

Mark Twain

I have certainly seen more men destroyed by the desire to have a wife and child and to keep them in comfort than I have seen destroyed by drink or harlots.

William Butler Yeats

Men have children to prove they aren't impotent, or at least that some of their friends aren't.

P. J. O'Rourke

When my son, Jake, was born, one of my first thoughts was oh good, someone to go to football matches with.

Hunter Davies

Warren Beatty only had children so he can meet some babysitters.

David Letterman

Children are the only form of immortality that we can be sure of.

Peter Ustinov

A son of my own! Oh, no, no, no! Let my flesh perish with me, and let me not transmit to anyone the boredom and the ignominiousness of life.

Gustave Flaubert

I don't like children, but I like to make them.

Groucho Marx

Parenting, there's a tough job. Easy job to get though. I think most people love the interview. You don't even have to dress for it.

Steve Bruner

I like children. Properly cooked.

W.C. Fields

Of children, as of procreation – the pleasure momentary, the posture ridiculous, the expense damnable.

Evelyn Waugh

He that doth get a wench with child and marries her afterwards it is as if a man should shit in his hat and then clap it on his head.

Samuel Pepys

I abominate the sight of children so much that I have always had the greatest regard for the character of Herod.

Lord Byron

My husband is English and I'm American. I wonder what our children would be like. They'd probably be rude, but disgusted by their own behaviour.

Rita Rudner

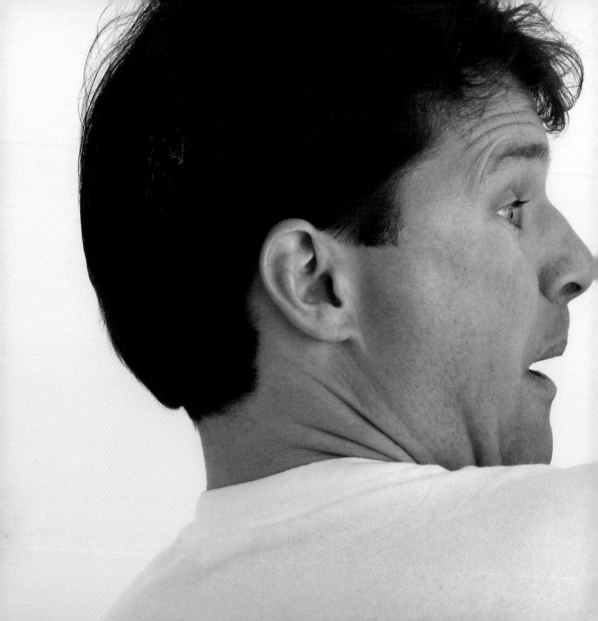

– Norm, how come you and Vera never had any kids?
– I can't, Coach.
– Gee, I'm sorry, Norm.
– I look at Vera … and I just can't.

'Coach' Pantusso and Norm Peterson, Cheers

I never want to get married and have children because I wouldn't want another me.

Simon Cowell

Literature is mostly about having sex and not much about having children. Life is the other way round.

David Lodge

I really want to have a child because Christmas without one is rubbish.

Hugh Grant

The time not to become a father is 18 years before a world war.

E.B. White

My views on birth control are somewhat distorted by the fact that I was the seventh of nine children.

Robert F. Kennedy

Never have children, only grandchildren.

Gore Vidal

My husband and I have discovered a foolproof method of birth control. An hour with the kids before bedtime.

Roseanne Barr

Oh, what a tangled web we weave when first we practise to conceive.

Don Herold

Don't you just hate those couples who go round telling everybody that they're 'trying' for a baby. We can do without the visual.

Pete Brown

Every sperm is sacred,
Every sperm is great;
If a sperm is wasted,
God gets quite irate.

Father, **Monty Python's The Meaning of Life**

Great Expectations

PREGNANCY

– We're going to have a baby. That's my Christmas present to you.
– All I needed was a tie.

Woody Allen

I assumed, prior to the experience, that I would be the most unlikely father. When Paula rang me and I was in New York she was blabbing, saying, 'Oh, I'm pregnant,' and I went 'Oh fuck!' but I didn't actually say that. I said, 'That's fantastic!' I just stared at myself in the mirror and kept saying, 'What the fuck now? You're going to be a father.' But then I wondered would I do all right? I knew it was the long haul, and I thought, 'Why not? And what better babe to do it with? It's going to be a hoot!'

Bob Geldof

I'd been cast in the part of my life … but I'd never heard of the leading man. I was definitely playing a supporting role. Still, I'd never had a better part, and only once one as good – in the sequel. I was to be a father!

Charlton Heston

It's not easy to juggle a pregnant wife and a troubled child, but somehow I manage to fit in eight hours of TV a day.

Homer Simpson

I do wish my husband would stop calling me Madame Ovary.

Alice Kane

I'm preparing for the baby. I'm busy putting childproof caps on all the bottles of booze.

David Letterman

When she was pregnant, my wife's craving was not to be pregnant.

Jez Tyler

Unto Us a Child Is Born

BIRTH

He became a father today. There'll be hell to pay if his wife finds out.

Milton Berle

Just as I was about to give birth, Mick arrived at the hospital bearing diamond earrings and caviar. The wives and nurses were very excited to find him there with a pot of caviar, and asked for lemon slices and toast.

Jerry Hall, ex-Mrs Jagger

Should a father be present at the birth of his child? It's all any reasonable child can expect if Dad is present at the conception.

Joe Orton

Men come into the delivery room and say, 'Breathe.' Is that really a sharing experience? If I ever have a baby I want my husband to be on the table next to me, at least getting his legs waxed.

Rita Rudner

I was fully prepared for being present at the birth of my first child: I watched the movie Alien a couple of times.

Bob Hayden

If men could get pregnant, abortion would be a sacrament.

Florynce Kennedy

You have this myth, as the father, that if you're there at the birth, you're sharing the birthing experience. Unless you're circumcising yourself with a chain saw, I don't think so. Unless you're opening an umbrella up your ass, I don't think so.

Robin Williams

– We have a new baby, can you guess what it is?
– A boy.
– No, guess again.

Gracie Allen and George Burns

The first handshake in life is the greatest of all: the clasp of an infant's fist around a parent's finger.

Mark Beltaire

I remember the very first time I ever held my son in my arms as a newborn. Everything else in the universe melted away. There was just a father, a son, and the distant sound of my wife saying, 'If you ever come near me again, I'll drop you with a deer rifle.'

Frasier Crane, **Frasier**

I married your mother because I wanted children. Imagine my disappointment when you came along.

Groucho Marx

Fortunately, my parents were intelligent, enlightened people. They accepted me for what I was, a punishment from God.

David Steinberg

You Must Have Been a Beautiful Baby

All babies are supposed to look like me – at both ends.

Winston Churchill

I was so ugly at birth that the midwife took one look at me, turned, and slapped my father.

Joan Rivers

I can see that it is a very homely baby indeed. Still I never see many babies that I consider rose geraniums for looks, anyway.

Damon Runyon

Introduced to his child, he recoiled with a startled 'Oi!' The only thing that prevented a father's love from faltering was the fact that there was in his possession a photograph of himself at the same early age, in which he, too, looked like a homicidal fried egg.

P.G. Wodehouse

Thank goodness he hasn't got ears like his father!

Queen Elizabeth II, on first seeing Prince William

In the Name of the Father

CHOOSING A NAME

Naming our baby was a trial. I seize up when I have to
name a document on my computer.

Jeff Stilson

Always end the name of your child with a vowel, so that
when you yell, the name will carry.

Bill Cosby

Donald Trump says he named his daughter Tiffany after his
favourite store, Tiffany's. How ridiculous is that? I was
saying so to my twins, Bargain and Booze.

Les Curtis

If you're gonna be a boxer, you gotta prepare for memory
loss. So I named all my kids George. Including the girls.

George Foreman

My dad's so sweet. He named his first ulcer after me.

Ellie Firth

High Hopes

When my son was born, I had a dream that one day he might grow up to win a Nobel Prize. But I had another dream that he might grow up to say, 'Do you want fries with that?'

Robin Williams

Dad had such high hopes for Vanessa and Corin but I was the one of whom nothing was expected. I remember a game the three of us played: Vanessa was the President of the United States, Corin was the British Prime Minister – and I was the royal dog.

Lynn Redgrave

When you become a parent, it is your biggest chance to grow again. You have another crack at yourself.

Fred Rogers

May you build a ladder to the stars and climb on every rung.

Bob Dylan

Bringing Up Baby

I'm 484 months old. Can you tell I'm a new father?

Reno Goodale

I used to think that having a dog was adequate preparation for parenthood, but I'm told they're not exactly the same, pet ownership and child rearing.

Paul Reiser

A baby is an alimentary canal with a loud voice at one end and no sense of responsibility at the other.

Ronald Knox

A baby is the most complicated object made by unskilled labour.

Steven Wright

Babies are the enemies of the human race.

Isaac Asimov

The toughest job in the world isn't being a President. It's being a parent.

Bill Clinton

People often ask me, 'What's the difference between couplehood and babyhood?' In a word? Moisture. Everything in my life is now more moist. Between your spittle, your diapers, your spit-up and drool, you got your baby food, your wipes, your formula, your leaky bottles, sweaty baby backs, and numerous other untraceable sources − all creating an ever-present moistness in my life, which heretofore was mainly dry.

Paul Reiser

I'm terrified of raising a kid. I can't even keep my plants alive.

Bill Maher

All children alarm their parents, if only because you are forever expecting to encounter yourself.

Gore Vidal

−Yeah, sure, for you, a baby's all fun and games. For me, it's diaper changes and midnight feedings.
− Doesn't Mom do all that stuff?
−Yeah, but I have to hear about it.

Homer and Lisa Simpson

The problem with men is that after the birth, we're irrelevant.

Dustin Hoffman

I was in analysis for years because of a traumatic childhood: I was breastfed through falsies.

Woody Allen

Actually what I've been surprised about in becoming a father is the lack of character that the baby has. It just lies there.

Guy Ritchie on baby Rocco

A Father's Lot Is Not a Nappy One

In the eyes of a mother, there is one single determining factor as to whether her husband is a good father or not: does he change the baby's nappy?

Anon

My friend's baby had an accident in its diaper. The mother comes over and says, 'Oh, how adorable. Brandon made a gift for Daddy.' I'm thinking this guy must be real easy to shop for on Father's Day.

Garry Shandling

When it comes to changing diapers there's only one thing to remember: never scratch and sniff.

David Letterman

Baby caca is like Kryptonite to a father. The dog's looking at you going, 'You don't rub his face in it.'

Robin Williams

Child-rearing

Kids are great. You can teach them to hate the things you hate and they practically raise themselves nowadays, you know, with the Internet and all.

Homer Simpson

How children survive being brought up amazes me.

Malcolm Forbes

Everybody knows how to raise children except the people who have them.

P. J. O'Rourke

All kids need is a little help, a little hope, and somebody who believes in them.

Earvin 'Magic' Johnson

All I heard when I was growing up was, 'Why can't you be more like your cousin Sheila? Why can't you be more like your cousin Sheila?' Sheila died at birth.

Joan Rivers

Teach your child to hold his tongue; he'll learn fast enough
to speak.

Benjamin Franklin

There is a horrible idea, beginning with Rousseau, that natural
man is naturally good. Anybody who's ever met a toddler knows
this is nonsense.

P. J. O'Rourke

There's only two things a child will share willingly –
communicable diseases and his mother's age.

Dr Benjamin Spock

A child is a curly, dimpled lunatic.

Ralph Waldo Emerson

Adam and Eve had many advantages, but the principal one was
that they escaped teething.

Mark Twain

The most popular question for small children is 'Why?'
They can use it anywhere and it's usually impossible to answer:
CHILD: What's that?
YOU: It's a goat.
CHILD: Why?

Dave Barry

Why is it that when you let a 3-year-old dress herself, she always dresses like an East European prostitute – pink tights, pink dress, pink shoes, little plaits and bright red lipstick?

David Baddiel

I have just returned from a children's party. I am one of the few survivors.

Percy French

As soon as I stepped out of my mother's womb on to dry land, I realized that I had made a mistake – that I shouldn't have come; but the trouble with children is that they are not returnable.

Quentin Crisp

The child was a keen bed-wetter.

Noël Coward

My father's sonorous voice brought Kipling's 'great greygreen, greasy Limpopo River all set about with fever-trees' snaking right to the foot of my bed.

Victoria Secunda

Never let a child wearing Superman pyjamas sleep on the top bunk.

Anon

There's so much crap talked about bringing up a child. A fucking moron could do it. Morons do bring up their children. It's just endless love, endless patience, that's it.

Bob Geldof

In the old days, of course, the Free World had an excellent system of high-quality, low-cost child care, namely your mother.

Dave Barry

I understand the importance of bondage between parent and child.

Dan Quayle

The end product of child-raising is not the child but the parent.

Frank Pittman

Childhood is a time when kids prepare to become grownups, so to get them ready for the real world, I think it makes sense to totally traumatize your children.

George Carlin

I was in the garden with my 3-year-old daughter, Honey, who was blowing bubbles. The sun was shining, the birds were singing, she turned to me and said, 'Daddy, my life is bubbles.' I thought, how lovely, then I snatched the bubbles from her little hand and threw them away. Because you've gotta teach kids that life can be unfair. You've gotta teach kids the arbitrariness of existence.

Jonathan Ross

My parents raised me with the three magic words: total sensory deprivation.

Emo Philips

I'd like to smack smug parents who say, 'Our 3-year-old's reading Harry Potter.' Well, my 3-year-old's smearing his shit on the fridge door.

Jack Dee

Teach your child to hold his tongue; he'll learn fast enough to speak.

Benjamin Franklin

It is no wonder people are so horrible when they started life as children.

Kingsley Amis

All women should know how to take care of children. Most of them will have a husband some day.

Franklin P. Jones

I love giving the kids a bath. There's great satisfaction in it. They get so dirty.

Curtis Black

A house is never perfectly furnished for enjoyment unless there is
a child in it rising 3 years old, and a kitten rising 3 weeks old.

Robert Southey

After a long day caring for our three kids, my wife had reached
the end of her tether. She was teary and cranky. My son said,
'Daddy, is she teething?'

Craig Ackland

The quickest way for a parent to get a child's attention is to sit
down and look comfortable.

Lane Olinghouse

A child of 3 cannot raise its chubby fist to its mouth to remove a
piece of carpet which it is through eating, without being made the
subject of a psychological seminar of child welfare experts.

Robert Benchley

For toddlers I suggest leaving their mittens on year round, indoors
and out. That way they can't get into aspirin bottles, liquor
cabinets or boxes of kitchen matches. Also, it keeps their little
hands clean for mealtimes.

P. J. O'Rourke

Kids do say the darndest things, but that's once in a blue moon,
and in between it's a lot of drivel.

Bill Maher

He uses my body for nine months like it's an all-you-can-eat salad bar and his first word is, 'Dada.'

Beth Cox, **Rock Me Baby**

I'm guessing Brooklyn Beckham's first words were Gucci, Gucci, goo.

Polly Stone

I grew up in a political family. The first words I spoke as a child were Mommy, Daddy, and Constituency.

Pat Robertson

A Brief Guide to Baby-talk: Takes after his father: Snores and suffers from wind; No trouble at all: We have a nanny; Loves books: Sucks them; Advanced for his age: Likes a drop of gin in his milk; Loveable: Fat.

John Koski and Mitchell Symons

If a kid asks where rain comes from, I think a cute thing to tell them is, 'God is crying.' And if they ask why God is crying, another cute thing to tell them is, 'Probably because of something you did.'

Jack Handey

My kid's endless questions are driving me crazy … why, why, why? Why didn't I pull out?

Steve McGrew

Children seldom misquote you. They more often repeat word for word what you shouldn't have said.

Mae Maloo

We had my boss and his wife over for dinner and my 4-year-old insisted on saying goodnight. As my boss's wife was patting him on the head, he said, 'My daddy wears Homer Simpson pants and farts in bed.' Bye bye promotion.

Mitch Goldberg

How to throw a children's party: dig a pit, throw in the kids and ice cream, add chocolate sauce; an hour later take out and send home.

Tony Kornheiser

In stark contrast to grown-up parties, partygoers at children's parties don't become embarrassingly drunk. It is the birthday-boy's or girl's father who becomes embarrassingly drunk.

Jeremy Hardy

Any child's birthday party in which the number of guests exceeds the number of the actual age of the child for whom the party is being given will end in disaster.

Pierre Burton

Hosting your child's party is like an exercise in riot control. Suddenly you find yourself spotting the ring leaders, appealing to the more moderate children to try and keep order, abandoning the living room to the mob and trying to consolidate your power base in the kitchen.

Jeremy Hardy

– He's more like his father every day.
– He sure is. This morning he was playing with a corkscrew.

Nora Charles and Stella, Shadow of the Thin Man

To our parents, we seem always to be works-in-progress.

Frank Pittman

Parents are the bones upon which children sharpen their teeth.

Peter Ustinov

Don't try to make your children grow up to be like you or they may do it.

Russell Baker

If you cannot open a childproof bottle, use pliers or ask a child.

Bruce Lansky

My parents never wanted me to get upset about anything. They couldn't tell me when a pet had died. One day I woke up and my goldfish had gone. I said, 'Where's Fluffy?' They said, 'He ran away.'

Rita Rudner

I try to raise my kids to be generous and sharing. The other day, my 3-year-old daughter offered me her bag of sweets and said, 'Take a lot. Take two.'

Edward Price

Closely he cuddled up to me,
And put his hand in mine,
Till all at once I seemed to be
Afloat on seas of brine.
Sabean odours clogged the air
And filled my soul with dread,
Yet I could only grin and bear
When Willie wet the bed.

Eugene Field

I found this priceless piece of advice in a childcare book dated 1595: 'A mouse roasted and given to children to eat remedieth pissing the bed.' So now you know.

Reg Collins

If you wonder where your child left his roller skates, try walking around the house in the dark.

Leopold Fechtner

Have you seen those toilet-training books? There's the popular, Everybody Poops; or the less popular, Nobody Poops But You; or, for Catholics, You're a Naughty, Naughty Boy and That's Concentrated Evil Coming Out of Your Bottom.

Peter Griffin, Family Guy

Training children is mostly a matter of pot luck.

Bob Monkhouse

I was watching Peter Pan with my 6-year-old daughter and she says, 'Daddy, how does Captain Hook wipe his bottom?' I just said, 'Smee does it.'

Bob Saget

I loved those years of being Mr Mom. One of the saddest days in my life was when Jennifer said, 'Dad, I can wash my own hair.'

Billy Crystal

– Dad, look at me.
– But if I pay attention to you, I have to stop watching TV. You can see the bind I'm in.

Bart and Homer Simpson

By the age of 6, the average child will have completed the basic American education. From television, the child will have learned how to pick a lock, commit a fairly elaborate hold-up, prevent wetness all day long, get the laundry twice as white, and kill people with a variety of sophisticated armaments.

Anon

When I was a kid, I would ask my dad if I could watch TV and he'd always say, 'Yes, but don't turn it on.'

Fragger, b3ta.com

Try treating your dog the way America treats its kids. Give the puppy her own set of house keys and put her in front of the television instead of taking her for a walk. Let her eat anything she wants and house train herself. Send her to another master for visitation at the weekends. And when she comes into heat, turn her loose in the pound.

P. J. O'Rourke

Parents exist to be grown out of.

John Wolfenden

Being a father is harder than being a rock 'n' roll singer on the road because any second your kid will run through the door with a 16-inch nail sticking through his head, going, 'Daddy, daddy, I just got hit by a 4x2.'

Ozzy Osbourne

The myriad disasters I envisaged for my own children in early life, such as contact with runaway juggernauts, rabid squirrels or molesting adults, were by some miracle successfully bypassed.

Robert Morley

The worst thing that can happen to a man is to have his wife come home and he has lost the child. 'How did everything go?' 'Just great, we're playing hide and seek and she's winning.'

Sinbad

My son Lawrie ran to me in tears. 'What's wrong?' I said. 'I stubbed my toe,' he wept. I took a closer look and asked which one hurt. Lawrie said, 'The one that ate roast beef.'

David Best

Being a father is the hardest job in the world. You try to lead your kids up the right path, but who am I to lead anybody up any fucking path? How can I give out the rules when I'm worse than them most of the time? When you see me coming home in police cars, in fucking ambulances, in straitjackets and chains?

Ozzy Osbourne

The essential skill of parenting is making up answers. When an experienced father is driving down the road and his kid asks how much a certain building weighs, he doesn't hesitate for a second. '3,457 tons,' he says.

Dave Barry

Son, I don't want you to do that because I don't want Mom to
worry, all right? When she worries she starts saying things like, 'I
told you so,' or 'Stop doing that, I'm asleep.'

Peter Griffin, **Family Guy**

A bathroom is a place where your child doesn't need to go until
you're backing your car out of the driveway.

Anon

What it really means to be a parent is: you will spend an
enormous portion of your time lurking outside public toilet stalls.
Children almost never have to go to the bathroom when they are
within a few miles of their own home toilets. Then, when you
get where they're going, let's say a restaurant, the child will wait
until your entrées arrive, then announce that they have to go. If
it is an especially loathsome bathroom that has not been cleaned
since the fall of Rome, the child will immediately announce that
they have to do a Number Two.

Dave Barry

In the end the negative aspects of being a parent – the loss of
intimacy, the expense, the total lack of free time, the incredible
responsibility, etc. – are more than outweighed by the positive
aspects, such as never again lacking for primitive drawings to
attach to your refrigerator with magnets.

Dave Barry

I bought a beautiful new fridge with a stainless steel door. It came with a spray so that children's paintings won't stick to it. Because you don't want it ruined, do you? 'That's nothing like a rocket, that.' Still, you have to compromise. The kids wanted fridge magnets. I said, 'Okay, but only one, and I choose.' I chose a life-size picture of a fridge door.

Jack Dee

Infants need the most sleep, and, what is more, get it. Stunning them with a soft, padded hammer is the best way to ensure their getting it at the right times.

Robert Benchley

If your child refuses to go to sleep, try acting out a nursery rhyme – Rockabye Baby always works for me.

David Letterman

I was reading Bible stories to my young son at bedtime … 'The man named Lot was warned to take his wife and flee out of the city but his wife looked back and was turned to salt.' My son sat up suddenly and said, 'What happened to the flea?'

Jason Wilson

– Daddy, tell me a story.
– Life stinks, The End.

Robbie and Earl Sinclair, **Dinosaur**

When I was a kid, I used to imagine animals running under my bed. I told my dad, and he solved the problem quickly. He cut the legs off my bed.

Lou Brock

Always kiss your children goodnight – even if they're already asleep.

H. Jackson Brown Jr

Will I Ever Have Sex Again?

– Could you knock before entering our bedroom?
– Like I'm gonna walk in on anything …

**Kerry and Paul Hennessy, 8 Simple Rules for Dating
My Teenage Daughter**

Children always assume the sexual lives of their parents come to a grinding halt at their conception.

Alan Bennett

– Having sex with a pregnant woman is like putting gas in a car you just wrecked.
– Well, luckily Peggy pulls into self-service.

Jefferson and Al Bundy, Married … With Children

Sex during pregnancy – sometimes the foetus joined in and jived about a bit, so it was like doing it with someone else in the room.

Michael Rosen

I could have been sexually abused, but after I was born my parents were hardly interested in having sex with each other.

P. J. O'Rourke

After you've had children sex slows down. We have sex every three months now. Every time I have sex, the next day, I pay my quarterly taxes. Unless it's oral sex, then I renew my driver's licence.

Ray Romano

I've learned that as a parent, when you have sex, your body emits a hormone that drifts down the hall into your child's room and makes them want a drink of water.

Jeff Foxworthy

My mother said the best time to ask my dad for anything was when he was having sex. Not the best advice I've ever been given.

Jimmy Carr

When I caught my parents having sex, my dad looked at me and just said one thing: 'It's more fun than it looks.'

Eric Foreman, **That 70s Show**

I could never take condoms seriously after the experience as a toddler of finding one of Daddy's special balloons under my parents' bed and taking it in turns with a small friend to blow it up. I never was taken with the smell of hot rubber, anyway.

Julie Walters

Fathers and Family Life

Now remember. As far as anyone knows, we're a nice normal family.

Homer Simpson

Every family has a secret, and the secret is that it's not like other families.

Alan Bennett

The family – that dear octopus from whose tentacles we never quite escape, nor, in our innermost hearts, ever quite wish to.

Dodie Smith

Father, Mother, and Me,
Sister and Auntie say
All the people like us are We,
And everyone else is They.

Rudyard Kipling

Where does the family start? It starts with a young man falling in love with a girl – no superior alternative has yet been found.

Winston Churchill

A family is a unit composed not only of children but of men, women, an occasional animal, and the common cold.

Ogden Nash

Fathers should be neither seen nor heard. That is the only proper basis for family life.

Oscar Wilde

The place of the father in the modern suburban family is a very small one, particularly if he plays golf.

Bertrand Russell

Having a family is like having a bowling alley installed in your brain.

Martin Mull

Our family didn't exactly come from the wrong side of the tracks, but we were certainly always within the sound of the train whistles.

Ronald Reagan

You're probably a redneck if your family tree doesn't fork.

Jeff Foxworthy

She's descended from a long line that her mother was once silly enough to listen to.

Gypsy Rose Lee

I don't know who my grandfather was; I am much more concerned to know what his grandson will be.

Abraham Lincoln

A Hollywood aristocrat is anyone who can trace his
ancestry back to his father.

Jay Leno

Ashes to ashes and clay to clay; if the enemy don't get you,
your own folk may.

James Thurber

Blood is thicker than water and much more difficult to get
out of the carpet.

Woody Allen

If murder had been allowed when dad was in his prime, our
home would have been like the last act of Othello almost
daily.

Nancy Mitford

Insanity runs in my family. It practically gallops.

Cary Grant

They were a tense and peculiar family, the Oedipuses,
weren't they?

Max Beerbohm

Home is the place there's no place like.

Charles Schulz

Size Matters

HOW BIG IS YOUR FAMILY?

I was the youngest of five boys. With so many brothers, my father bought us a dachshund so we could all pet him at the same time.

Bob Hope

The great advantage of living in a large family is that early lesson of life's essential unfairness.

Nancy Mitford

Having one child makes you a parent; having two you are a referee.

David Frost

Children are like pancakes: you should always throw out the first one.

Peter Benchley

I'm an only child, although I did have an imaginary friend – who my parents actually preferred.

Chandler Bing, Friends

Mum, Dad, Same Difference?

Mothers are a biological necessity; fathers are a social invention.

Margaret Mead

A woman knows everything about her children. She knows about dental appointments and football games and best friends and favourite foods and romances and secret fears and hopes and dreams. A man is vaguely aware of some short people living in the house.

Dave Barry

If my father was the head of the house, my mother was its heart.

Huw, **How Green Was My Valley**

The reason why mothers are more devoted to their children than fathers is that they suffer more in giving them birth and are more certain that they are their own.

Aristotle

My mother protected me from the world and my father threatened me with it.

Quentin Crisp

Some Great Things About Being a Dad

Anyone who hasn't had children doesn't know what life is.

Henry Miller

I don't need stuff like pot or booze. My high is my wife and kids.

Bill Cosby

Children are a great investment. They beat the hell out of stocks.

Peter Lynch

Children make you want to start life over.

Muhammad Ali

If all the world thought and acted like children, we'd never have any trouble. The only pity is even kids have to grow up.

Walt Disney

Fathers Observed

My father was a man of great principle, though what those principles were I cannot say.

Eugene O'Neill

My father was a relentlessly self-improving boulangerie owner from Belgium with low-grade narcolepsy and a penchant for buggery. He would womanize, he would drink. He would make outrageous claims like he invented the question mark.

Dr Evil, **Austin Powers**

My dad was a kind of father figure to me.

Alan Coren

Mom and Pop were just a couple of kids when they got married. He was 18, she was 16 and I was 3.

Billie Holiday

If you have not had a good father, it is necessary to invent one.

Friedrich Nietzsche

Your father was Frankenstein, but your mother was the lightning.

Bela Lugosi, **The Ghost of Frankenstein**

Your mother was a hamster, and your father smelt of elderberries.

French Soldier, **Monty Python and the Holy Grail**

I just got this telegram from daddy. Ten words exactly. After ten, it's extra. Daddy thinks of these things. If I had leprosy, there'd be a cable: 'Gee, kid, tough. Sincerely hope nose doesn't drop off. Love.'

Sally Bowles, **Cabaret**

My father was not a failure. After all, he was the father of the President of the United States.

Harry S. Truman

What's it like to be the son of the President of the United States? That's like asking a tomato how it feels to be red.

Ronald Reagan Jr

Children begin by loving their parents. After a time they judge them. Rarely, if ever, do they forgive them.

Oscar Wilde

Nothing has a stronger influence psychologically on their environment, and especially on their children, than the unlived life of the parents.

Carl Jung

My kids hate me. They keep leaving phone numbers of divorce lawyers in Mom's purse.

David Letterman

Mr Fixit

DIY DADS

My dad, he'd try anything – carpentry, electrical wiring, plumbing, roofing. From watching him, I learned that no matter how difficult a task may seem, if you're not afraid to try it, you can do it. And when you're done, it will leak.

Dave Barry

My dad is Mr Fixit. He cruises the house with a screwdriver in his hand looking for something to tighten.

Rod Lake

– Dad's fixing the dryer.
– Oh dear, you know, ever since the plant cut back his hours, he's spent all his time fixing things. Things that don't need fixing. Things I need, things I use, things I love. I gotta go hide the crock pot.

Eric and Kitty Foreman, **That 70s Show**

My dad's one of those Mr Fixit guys. Every Sunday morning he'd be locked down in the basement with the power tools. When my sister got married, we had to lead him into the church with a broken toaster.

Mike Rowe

Daddy, Can We Play Monopoly?

FUN, GAMES AND SPORT

I knew I was an unwanted baby when I saw that my bath toys
were a toaster and a radio. My parents gave me a rattle that was
still attached to the snake.

Joan Rivers

My parents put a live teddy bear in my crib.

Woody Allen

Everyone who ever walked barefoot into his child's room late at
night hates Lego.

Tony Kornheiser

One time I had to go out, so I asked Woody Allen to watch
the children. When I returned less than an hour later, he was
throwing his hats and gloves into the fire. The kids were ecstatic.
Woody just shrugged and said, 'I ran out of things to do.'

Mia Farrow

Children's Books That Didn't Make It: You Were an Accident;
Hammers, Screwdrivers and Scissors: An I-Can-Do-It Book;
Some Kittens Can Fly; That's It, I'm Putting You Up for
Adoption; Strangers Have the Best Candy; Things Rich Kids
Have, But You Never Will; Daddy Drinks Because You Cry.

Anon

My father took me to the zoo. He told me to go over to the
leopard and play connect the dots.

Rodney Dangerfield

When I was a kid, I asked my dad if I could go ice-skating. He
told me to wait until it gets warmer.

Rodney Dangerfield

When you give a child a hammer, everything becomes a nail.

Leo Kaplan

Father's Day

Father's Day is the same as Mother's Day but you don't spend as much.

Bill Cosby

Father's Day is the day when father goes broke giving his family money so they can surprise him with gifts he doesn't need.

Richard Taylor

My kids hate me. Every Father's Day they give a 'World's Greatest Dad' mug to the milkman.

Rodney Dangerfield

I hate Father's Day because I can never find the right card. They're all too nice.

Margaret Smith

Last year on Father's Day, my son gave me something I've always wanted: the keys to my car.

Al Sterling

What Dads Say

How many times do I have to tell you?
I don't care what 'everyone' is doing.
Are you deaf or something?
I don't care who else is going.
Do you think I'm made of money?
Who'll end up feeding it and taking it for a walk?
Money doesn't grow on trees.
After all we do for you.
You don't know how lucky you are.
I hope someday you have kids just like you.
How do you know you don't like it if you haven't tasted it?
Don't speak with your mouth full.
Don't sit so close to the television.
I won't tell you again.
I didn't ask who put it there, I said, 'Pick it up.'
If I've told you once, I've told you a thousand times.
It must be somewhere.
Is that what you're going to wear?
Over my dead body.
Because I say so, that's why.
Someday you'll thank me.
What did I just say?
Stop crying or I'll give you something to cry about.

Wipe your shoes before you come through that door.
Take your feet off the sofa.
You'll have someone's eye out with that.
Don't ever let me catch you doing that again.
Don't get smart with me.
When I was a little boy …
Get a haircut!
You have enough dirt in your ears to grow potatoes.
You take after your mother.
Don't come crying to me.
Do it to make your mother happy.
If the wind changes, you'll stay that way.
You're old enough to know better.
Wait till you have children of your own.
It's such a lovely day. Why don't you go and play in the
garden? Oh, take the rubbish to the bin while you're at it.
As long as you live under my roof, you'll do as I say.
Because I'm your father, that's why.
Close the door! You don't live in a barn.
You'd better ask your mother.

Things you won't hear a father say: 'Go ahead, take my car –
and here's 50 bucks for gas'; 'Here, you take the remote';
'Can you turn up that music? It really calms my nerves';
'Waiter! More ice cream for the little one!'

David Letterman

I Want it Now!

SPOILT BRATS

– I want it now, Daddy!

– Veruca, sweetheart, I'm not a magician.

– You're a rotten, mean father. You never give me anything I want.

Veruca and Henry Salt,
Willy Wonka and the Chocolate Factory

– You're bribing your daughter with a car?

– Ah, c'mon, isn't 'bribe' just another word for 'love'?

Lois and Peter Griffin, **Family Guy**

The thing that impresses me most about America is the way the parents obey their children.

Duke of Windsor

I have never seen a happy spoilt child or adult.

Tom Lacey

Whenever I mentioned to my father that I wanted a television set, his stock reply was, 'People in Hell want ice water.'

Garrison Keillor

I'd like to thank my parents for giving me the gift of poverty.

Roberto Begnini, in his Oscar acceptance speech

Your children need your presence more than your presents.

Jesse Jackson

My father was always carrying me in his arms, giving me loud, moist kisses and calling me pet names like 'little sparrow' and 'little fly'. Once I ruined a tablecloth with a pair of scissors. My mother spanked me across the hand until it hurt. I cried so hard that my father came and took me by the hand. He kissed me and comforted me and quieted me down.

Svetlana Aliluyeva on her father, Joseph Stalin

Wait 'til Your Father Gets Home

DISCIPLINE

Children today are tyrants. They have no respect for their elders, flout authority and have appalling manners. What terrible creatures will they grow up into?

Socrates

My wife and I have many things in common the greatest of which is that we are both afraid of the children.

Bill Cosby

The modern child will answer you back before you've said anything.

Laurence J. Peter

Speak roughly to your little boy,
And beat him when he sneezes;
He only does it to annoy,
Because he knows it teases.

Lewis Carroll

Don't go into Mr McGregor's garden: your father had an accident there; he was put in a pie by Mrs McGregor.

Beatrix Potter, **The Tale of Peter Rabbit**

I can do one of two things: I can be President of the United States or I can control Alice. I cannot possibly do both.

Theodore Roosevelt

There was a little girl
Who had a little curl
Right in the middle of her forehead.
When she was good
She was very very good
And when she was bad
She was horrid.

Mother Goose

Children of Progressive Parents Admitted Only on Leads.

Notice in London restaurant

My father was frightened of his father. I was frightened of my father, and I am damned well going to see to it that my children are frightened of me.

King George V

In dealing with my children I always keep one thing in mind: we're bigger than they are, and it's our house.

Moss Hart

Hey, just because I don't care doesn't mean I'm not listening.

Homer Simpson

O-oh, Junior's learned to say my 'Ouch-I-hit-my-thumb-with-the-hammer' word.

David Letterman

Children are never too tender to be whipped. Like tough beefsteaks, the more you beat them, the more tender they become.

Edgar Allan Poe

My father only hit me once. But he used a Volvo.

Bob Monkhouse

Children should be seen and not heard.

Aristophanes

My father is the most even-tempered man in the Navy: he is always in a rage.

Elizabeth King

No one used revenge better than my father. I always imagined that scene in The Godfather, where some guy wakes up with a horse head next to him, was probably my dad's idea of a get-well greeting card.

Ruby Wax

I remember the time I was kidnapped and they sent a piece of my finger to my father. He asked for more proof.

Rodney Dangerfield

My parents finally realize that I'm kidnapped and they snap into action immediately: they rent out my room.

Woody Allen

During the Blitz I was asked if I wanted to have my books or my son evacuated to the safety of the country. I chose my books because many of them were irreplaceable but I could always have another son.

Evelyn Waugh

Children are immune to stress but are carriers.

John Spender

Encouragement after censure is as the sun after a shower.

Johann Wolfgang von Goethe

Remember that children, marriages and flower gardens reflect the kind of care they get.

H. Jackson Brown Jr

You may be a pain in the ass, you may be bad, but child, you belong to me.

Ray Charles

Feeding the Mouth That Bites You

FOOD AND DRINK

There are times when parenthood seems nothing but feeding the mouth that bites you.

Peter de Vries

The book says to feed the baby every two hours, but do you count from when you start, or when you finish? It takes me two hours to get her to eat, and by the time she's done, it's time to start again, so that I'm feeding her all the time.

Peter Mitchell, **Three Men and a Baby**

Carrots? I don't know what company makes this stuff, but I hate it.

Dewey Wilkerson, **Malcolm in the Middle**

Son, if you don't eat your peas, your widget won't grow.

Gordon Ramsay, **Hell's Kitchen Revisited**

I loved giving breakfast to the girls, and I loved it after Abigail became old enough to understand that, remarkable as I was, I did not deserve total credit for making such good corn flakes.

Calvin Trillin

When I was a kid, my dad used to say to me, 'Eat your peas. It'll put hair on your chest.' I'm five. I'm Italian. I already have hair on my chest.

Maria Menozzi

I tell kids they should throw away the cereal and eat the box. At least they'd get some fibre.

Dr Richard Holstein

This would be a better world for children if parents had to eat the spinach.

Groucho Marx

My dad's so impatient. He stands in front of the microwave going, 'Come on! It's been ten seconds. I don't have all minute!'

Cathy Ladman

Never ask a three-year-old to hold a tomato.

Anon

Things you don't want to hear at your family barbecue: 'If you don't wash your hands, it gives the burgers more flavour'; 'Which do you want first, kids? Ice cream or the name of your real father?'

David Letterman

My dad skinned and cooked my pet rabbit, Blackie, for dinner.
We weren't that hard up. He just fancied a bit of rabbit.

Johnny Vegas

The other day I ate at a real nice family restaurant. Every
table had an argument going.

George Carlin

Do You Think I'm Made of Money?

MONEY MATTERS

Money isn't everything – but it sure keeps you in touch with your children.

John Paul Getty

I sometimes wish my father realized he was poor instead of being that most nerve-racking of phenomena, a rich man without money.

Peter Ustinov

A married man with a family will do anything for money.

Charles de Talleyrand

I was born in very sorry circumstances. My mother was sorry and my father was sorry as well.

Norman Wisdom

Saving is a fine thing. Especially when your parents have done it for you.

Winston Churchill

My dad was so cheap. When I was a kid and the ice cream van came round, he'd say, 'When they play the music, that means they've run out of ice cream.'

Bob Hayden

My dad's spending habits used to drive my mother up the wall. One moment he'd be buying her a diamond ring, the next he'd be bawling her out for not turning off the lights when she left the room.

Arthur Marx, son of Groucho

My husband is so cheap. On Christmas Eve he fires one shot and tells the kids Santa committed suicide.

Phyllis Diller

– Darling, when was the last time we received a letter from our son?
– Just a second, I'll look in the chequebook.

Anon

There are three books my daughter felt were the most important influences in her life: the Bible, her mother's cookbook and her father's chequebook.

Joyce Mattingly

If you want to recapture your youth, cut off his allowance.

Al Bernstein

A son could bear complacently the death of his father while the loss of his inheritance might drive him to despair.

Niccolò Machiavelli

I have never been a material girl. My father always told me never to love anything that cannot love you back.

Imelda Marcos

Life was a lot simpler when what we honoured was father and mother rather than all major credit cards.

Robert Orben

I haven't taught you anything about the value of money. Basically, it's worthless, but it lets you buy a lot of things that you can enjoy.

Ernest Hemingway

Behind the Wheel

THE FAMILY CAR

For Sale: 1993 Toyota Supra twin turbo, £14,250, very rare, every toy, traction, cruise, private number plate, 160 mph, awesome, girlfriend forgot to take pill, gutted.

Advert in **Autotrader** *magazine*

Children in back seats cause accidents. Accidents in back seat cause children.

Anon

Yeah, I know some people are against drunk driving – like cops for example. But, you know, sometimes, you've just got no choice: those kids gotta get to school.

Dave Attell

The problem with a 'Baby on Board' sign is that parents don't take it down when the baby isn't on board. They should have a sign saying, 'Baby at Auntie Jean's'. That way we'd know where the baby is so we could adjust our driving.

Arthur Smith

Are We There Yet?

TRAVEL

Are we there yet?

Perennial question child asks on getting in the car

A vacation is when the family goes away for a rest, accompanied by Mother, who sees that the others get it.

Marcelene Cox

Every year my family would pile into the car for our vacation and drive 80 trillion miles just to prove we couldn't get along in any setting.

Janeane Garofalo

A family vacation is one where you arrive with five bags, four kids and seven I-thought-you-packed-its.

Ivern Ball

There are two classes of travel – first class and with children.

Robert Benchley

Disneyland: purgatory, with better parking space.

Anon

Growing Up

As our children grow, so must we grow to meet their changing emotional, intellectual, and designer-footwear needs.

Dave Barry

She was growing up, and that was the direction I wanted her to take. Who wants a daughter that grows sideways?

Spike Milligan

Watching children grow up is a great delight. You see in them your own faults and your wife's virtues, and that can be a very stabilizing influence.

Peter Ustinov

I've noticed that one thing about parents is that no matter what stage your child is in, the parents who have older children always tell you the next stage is worse.

Dave Barry

My 11-year-old daughter mopes around the house all day waiting for her breasts to grow.

Bill Cosby

Boys do not grow up gradually. They move forward in spurts like the hands of the clocks in railway stations.

Cyril Connolly

You know your children are growing up when they stop asking where they came from and refuse to tell youwhere they're going.

P. J. O'Rourke

I can't decide whether growing pains are something kids have – or are.

Jackson Cole

Mother nature is wonderful. She gives us 12 years to develop a love for our children before turning them into teenagers.

Eugene Bertin

A pre-teen is sort of like having a tornado before a hurricane hits.

W. Bruce Cameron

The Clearasil Years

TEENAGERS

It's extraordinary. One day, you look at your phone bill and realize your child is a teenager.

Milton Berle

If Abraham's son had been a teenager, it wouldn't have been a sacrifice.

Scott Spendlove

Get Out of My Life, But First Could You Drive Me and Cheryl to the Mall: A Parent's Guide to the New Teenager

Anthony E. Wolf, book title

8 Simple Rules for Dating My Teenage Daughter and Other Tips for a Beleaguered Father (Not That Any of Them Work)

W. Bruce Cameron, book title

When your daughter is 12 she is given a splendidly silly article of clothing called a training bra. To train what? I never had a training jockstrap.

Bill Cosby

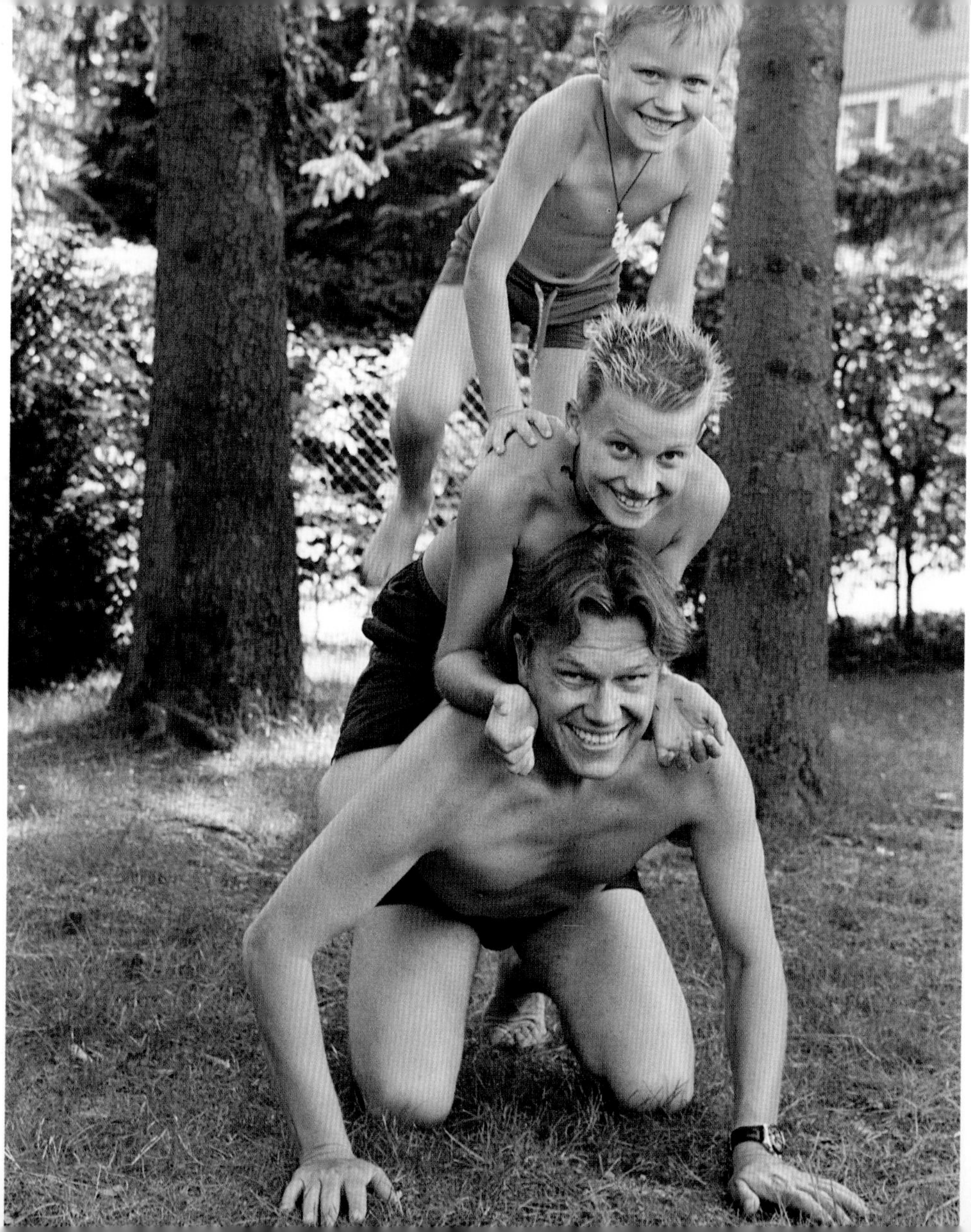

No need to worry about your teenagers when they're not at home. A national survey revealed that they all go to the place – 'out' – and they all do the same thing there –'nothing'.

Bruce Lansky

My daughter brought home one of her 'Goth' friends – black nail polish, black lipstick, black eyeliner, black hair, Liquid paper-white face. I'm sorry, didn't we use to call that 'Halloween'?

Jeff Foxworthy

That child was born gloomy. She named her guinea pigs 'Death' and 'Destruction'; she has an imaginary friend with leukaemia.

Carrie, Carrie and Barry

Have you ever found yourself sneaking into your teenage son's bedroom while he's at school to stare at his posters of nubile pop stars?

Clint Ferris

Adolescence is a time of rapid change. Between the ages of 12 and 17, for example, a parent can age as much as 20 years.

Anon

When I was a teenager, I used to try to make my head explode by holding my breath, thinking that if I blew up my head, my mom and dad would be sorry.

Kurt Cobain

As a psychiatrist, I can take comfort in the fact that without embarrassing parents, there'd be no psychology.

*Frasier Crane, **Frasier***

The other night, my little teenage daughter came home and said – and I don't think she was being very original – 'Daddy, as an outsider, how do you feel about the human race?'

Lyndon B. Johnson

If I'm more of an influence on your son as a rapper than you are as a father, you've got to look at yourself as a parent.

Ice Cube

When I was a boy of 14, my father was so ignorant I could hardly stand to have the old man around. But when I got to be 21, I was astonished at how much he had learned in seven years.

Mark Twain

We Don't Need No Education

School is where you go between when your parents can't
take you and industry can't take you.

John Updike

My very first day of school, my parents dropped me off atthe
wrong nursery. I didn't know anyone. And there were lots of trees.

Brian Kiley

My father wanted me to have all the educational opportunities
he never had so he sent me to a girls' school.

Eric Morecambe

Children are smarter than any of us. Know how I know that? I
don't know one child with a full-time job and children.

Bill Hicks

A child supplies the power but the parents have to do
the steering.

Dr Benjamin Spock

Every family should have at least three children. Then if one is a genius the other two can support him.

George Coote

I talk and talk and talk, and I haven't taught people in 50 years what my father taught me by example in one week.

Mario Cuomo

I learned the way a monkey learns – by watching my parents.

Prince Charles

One father is more than 100 schoolmasters.

George Herbert

When I read my son's report card all I could say in his favour was that with those grades, he couldn't possibly be cheating.

Jacob Braude

I will not allow my daughters to learn foreign languages because one tongue is sufficient for a woman.

John Milton

My kid drives me nuts. For three years now he's been going to a private school. He won't tell me where it is.

Rodney Dangerfield

One woman said to my father, Nat 'King' Cole: 'You know, we don't want any undesirables in this neighbourhood.' And my father just looked at her and said, 'Well, if I see any I'll let you know.'

Natalie Cole

As he waved me off to college, I'll never forget my dad's parting words. He said, 'Son, if there's anything you want, call me and I'll show you how to live without it.'

Will Collins

Driver Carries No Cash – He Has a Son in College.

Bumper sticker

The Birds and the Bees

SEX EDUCATION

These days when a father says, 'Son, I think it's time we had a little talk about sex,' the reply is apt to be, 'Okay, what did you want to know?'

Herbert Mumm

My father told me all about the birds and the bees, the liar – I went steady with a woodpecker till I was 21.

Bob Hope

Sex education was a dirty word when I was growing up. I didn't even know National Geographic ran pictures until I was married. Daddy always cut them out.

Erma Bombeck

The message about sex that she had got as a child was confused and contradictory. Sex was for men, and marriage, like lifeboats, was for women and children.

Carrie Fisher

My young son, Jack, asked me the dreaded question, 'Where do I come from, Daddy?' I decided not to fob him off, and gave him the full, frank explanation about sexual intercourse, orgasms and birth. 'Oh,' he said, 'I was just wondering, because the boy who sits in front of me comes from Jamaica.'

Paul LeBec

– ... and then Mommy kissed Daddy, and the angel told the stork, and the stork flew down from heaven, and put the diamond in the cabbage patch, and the diamond turned into a baby!
– Our parents are having a baby too. They had sex.

Little girl and Wednesday Addams, **Addams Family Values**

I didn't know the facts of life until I was 17. My father never talked about his work.

Martin Freud, son of Sigmund

Telling a teenager the facts of life is like giving a fish a bath.

Arnold Glasgow

Never come out to your father in a moving vehicle.

Kate Clinton

Dating

Red nail polish? Why don't we just buy you some rouge,
high heels and a lamppost?

Archie Bunker, All in the Family

When one of my daughter's boyfriends comes over to the house
I just say, 'See that little girl over there? She's my life. So if you
have any thoughts about hugging or kissing, you remember these
words: I've got no problem going back to prison.'

Bill Engvall

In high school, my sister went out with the captain of the chess
team. My mom and dad loved him. They figured that any guy
that took two hours to make a move was okay with them.

Brian Kiley

My dad told me, 'Marry a girl who has the same beliefs as the
family.' I said, 'Dad, why would I want to marry a girl who thinks
I'm a schmuck?'

Adam Sandler

Never date a woman whose father calls her 'Princess'. Chances
are she believes it.

Anon

My father used to say, 'Be home by midnight, or, by God, sleep on the porch!'

Oprah Winfrey

My fiancée's father said to me, 'If you're going to be my son-in-law, you need not go on calling me Sir. Call me Field Marshal.'

John Betjeman

One of life's greatest mysteries is how the boy who wasn't good enough to marry your daughter can be the father of the smartest grandchild in the world.

Anon

Following in Father's Footsteps

WORK

At the unemployment exchange, my father gave his occupation as an astronaut but not prepared to travel.

Roy Brown

For the first time in my life – I was then 11 years old – I felt myself forced into an open opposition. No matter how hard and determined my father might be about putting his own plans and opinions into action, his son was no less obstinate in refusing to accept ideas on which he set little or no value. I would not become a civil servant.

Adolf Hitler

Being a member of parliament is the sort of job all working-class parents want for their children – clean, indoors, and no heavy lifting.

Diane Abbott, MP

I remember when I took you for your first tetanus shot, son. You were about five or six. When the nurse gave you the shot, you took your mind off it by listing the names of all of Puccini's operas. Right then I knew you'd never be a cop like me.

Martin Crane, Frasier

Whatever happened to the good old days when children worked in factories?

Emo Philips

My father invented the burglar alarm, but it was stolen from him.

Victor Borge

William Pitt the Younger is not only a chip off the old block but the old block itself.

Edmund Burke

My father invented a cure for which there was no disease, and unfortunately, my mother caught it and died of it.

Victor Borge

Often Daddy sat up very late working on a case of Scotch.

Robert Benchley

I work as my father drank.

George Bernard Shaw

My dad was the town drunk. Usually that's not so bad, but New York City?

Henny Youngman

I just received the following wire from my generous daddy:
'Dear Jack, Don't buy a single vote more than is necessary. I'll be damned if I'm going to pay for a landslide.'

John F. Kennedy

My brother, Bob, doesn't want to be in government – he promised Dad he'd go straight.

John F. Kennedy

If I was an employer, I'd employ nothing but fathers – they always want an excuse to work late.

Julie Burchill

– My dad's a headhunter.
– Cool! Does he cut them off with a chainsaw?

Harry Gough and Tim Right, **The Right Stuff**

My father was a soldier who, after 30 years of service, was catapulted to the rank of corporal.

Woody Allen, **Take the Money and Run**

I used to eat quite a lot of fast food. When my daughter, Chelsea, started preschool and she was asked what her father did, she said that he worked at McDonald's.

Bill Clinton

My father said to me, 'Never do a job that can be replaced by machines.' So I thought being an actor was a job that can't be replaced by machines. But it looks as though we might be getting nearer to that stage.

Michael Caine

My mother said, 'You children must be extra polite to strangers because your father's an actor.'

Dorothy Fields

Every time I'm about ready to go to bed with a guy, I have to look at my dad's name all over the guy's underwear.

Marci Klein, daughter of Calvin Klein

The mill's closed, children. There's no more work. We're destitute. I'm afraid I have no choice but to sell you all for scientific experiments.

Father, **Monty Python's The Meaning of Life**

– Has fatherhood affected your song writing in any way?
– Well, it's harder to find the ashtrays.

Tom Waits

There is no more sombre enemy of art than the pram in the hall.

Cyril Connolly

Nobody ever asks a father how he manages to combine marriage and a career.

Sam Ewing

The average man will bristle if you say his father was dishonest, but he will brag a little if he discovers that his great-grandfather was a pirate.

Bern Williams

My father taught me to work; he did not teach me to love it. I never did like to work, and I don't deny it. I'd rather read, tell stories, crack jokes, talk, laugh – anything but work.

Abraham Lincoln

No man on his deathbed ever looked up into the eyes of his family and said, 'I wish I'd spent more time at the office.'

Anon

Our Father Who Art in Heaven

RELIGION

I am determined that my children shall be brought up in
their father's religion, if they can find out what it is.

Charles Lamb

At bottom, God is nothing more than an exalted father.

Sigmund Freud

And people tell me Jesus wasn't Jewish. Of course he was Jewish!
Thirty years old, still living at home with his parents, working in
his father's business, his mother thought he was God's gift …

Robin Williams

My parents raised me in the Jewish tradition. I was taught
never to marry a Gentile woman, shave on Saturday and, most
especially, never to shave a Gentile woman on Saturday.

Woody Allen

I do want to have Brooklyn christened, but I'm not sure
which religion.

David Beckham

It is almost nicer being a godfather than a father, like having white mice but making your nanny feed them for you.

T. H. White

My father considered a walk among the mountains as the equivalent of churchgoing.

Aldous Huxley

To impress upon us what the loss of the soul through mortal sin meant, my father would light a match, grab our hands and hold them briefly over the flame, saying, 'See how that feels? Now imagine that for all eternity.'

Pat Buchanan

Empty Nest

This is the hardest truth for a father to learn: that his children are continuously growing up and moving away from him (until, of course, they move back in).

Bill Cosby

I call my son the boomerang kid because he keeps on moving back.

Ross Cooper

There isn't a child who hasn't gone out into the brave new world who eventually doesn't return to the old homestead carrying a bundle of dirty clothes.

Art Buchwald

A Jewish man with parents still alive is a 15-year-old boy, and will remain a 15-year-old boy until they die.

Philip Roth

Though we have raised you for this moment of departure and we're very proud of you, a part of us longs to hold you once more as we did when you could barely walk – to read you just one more time Goodnight Moon.

Bill Clinton, at daughter Chelsea's high school graduation ceremony

Let your children go if you want to keep them.

Malcolm Forbes

I get along great with my parents. I still talk to them at least once a week. It's the least I can do. I still live in their house.

David Corrado

Human beings are the only creatures on earth that allow their children to come back home.

Bill Cosby

Papa Don't Preach

FATHERLY ADVICE

My father always said, 'Never write anything down that you wouldn't want published on the front page of the New York Times.'

Ted Kennedy

With my father there was no such thing as half-trying. Whether it was running a race or catching a football, competing in school – we were to try our best. 'After you have done the best you can,' he used to say, 'the hell with it.'

Robert F. Kennedy

Kennedys don't cry.

John F. Kennedy

Dad told all the boys to get laid as often as possible.

John F. Kennedy

'Never trust a man who doesn't drink,' was one of my father's favourite expressions, and he died plenty trustworthy.

Les Patterson

Never put anything on paper, my boy, and never trust a man with a small black moustache.

P.G. Wodehouse

As you journey through life, son, you will encounter all sorts of nasty little upsets, and you will either learn to adjust yourself to them or gradually go nuts.

Groucho Marx

Father told me if I ever met a lady in a dress like yours, I must look her straight in the eye.

Prince Charles

My father used to say, 'Never accept a drink from a urologist.'

Erma Bombeck

My dad told me, 'Don't go looking for trouble, but if you find it, make damn sure you win.'

John Wayne

Son, you tried to do something and you failed. What's the lesson here? Never try.

Homer Simpson

The most important thing parents can teach their children is how to get along without them.

Frank Clark

I owe a lot to my parents, especially my mother and father.

Greg Norman

My dad used to say, 'Always fight fire with fire,' which is probably why he was thrown out of the fire brigade.

Harry Hill

I phoned my dad to tell him I had stopped smoking. He called me a quitter.

Jo Brand

It was a maxim with our revered father – 'Always suspect everybody.'

Charles Dickens, **The Old Curiosity Shop**

When I was a small boy, my father told me never to recommend a church or a woman to anyone. And I have found it wise never to recommend a restaurant either. Something always goes wrong with the cheese soufflé.

Edmund Love

The best advice I was ever given was on my 21st birthday when my father said, 'Son, here's a million dollars. Don't lose it.'

Larry Niven

My dad said, 'You'll never be someone because you procrastinate.'
I said, 'Just you wait.'

Ted Carnes

My dad used to say, 'Keep your chin up, son.' He once broke his
jaw walking into a lamppost.

Adam Sandler

My father told me I should make a point of trying every
experience once – except incest and folk dancing.

Leo Fallon

Every father should remember that one day his son will follow
his example instead of his advice.

Anon

My father used to say, 'Let them see you and not the suit.
That should be secondary.'

Cary Grant

Around the time I made 9½ Weeks, I was doing lots of interviews
in which I talked frankly about sex. My dad sent me a can of
tennis balls with this note taped to it: 'Dear Kim, when you
give an interview and the feeling of being outrageous is present,
place one of these balls in your mouth. If you are still able to say
"oral sex" after doing this, then you are hopeless. Love from your
loving father better known as Daddy.'

Kim Basinger

My dad used to tell me, 'You're never as good as they say you are when they say you're good, and you're never as bad as they say you are when they say you're bad.' And once you understand that, you can survive.

George Clooney

My father, Denis, was fond of saying, 'Better to keep your mouth closed and be thought a fool than to open it and remove all doubt.'

Carol Thatcher

My dad always said, 'If you don't stand for something, you'll fall for anything.'

Jimmy Osmond

My dad, Tony Richardson, used to repeat a line of Samuel Beckett's so often that I had it pinned on my wall at home: 'Keep on failing. Only this time fail better.'

Joely Richardson

Always be a little kinder than necessary.

J. M. Barrie

Whenever I was in trouble, Dad would say, 'Step over the body and keep moving.'

Ralph Grigson

Dad always thought laughter was the best medicine, which I guess is why several of us died of tuberculosis.

Jack Handey

I've always followed my father's advice. He told me, first, to keep my word, and, second, to never insult anybody unintentionally. So if I insult you, you can be goddamn sure I intend to.

John Wayne

Son, you get out of it what you put into it.

Earl Woods

I remember my young brother once saying, 'I'd like to marry Elizabeth Taylor,' and my father said, 'Don't worry, your turn will come.'

Spike Milligan

How true Daddy's words were when he said, 'All children must look after their own upbringing.'

Anne Frank

Daddy's Little Girl

FATHERS AND DAUGHTERS

You have a girl. Unless I cut the wrong cord.

Dr Kosevich, Nine Months

What are little girls made of?
What are little girls made of?
Sugar and spice
And all things nice,
That's what girls are made of.

Nursery rhyme

It is only rarely that one can see in a little boy the promise
of a man, but one can almost always see in a little girl the
threat of a woman.

Alexandre Dumas

I only have two rules for my newly born daughter: she will dress
well; she will never have sex.

John Malkovich

I dedicate this book to my daughter Leonora without whose never-failing sympathy and encouragement it would have been finished in half the time.

P.G. Wodehouse

I was raised by my dad. When I was 13 and got my period, I had to tell him I needed tampons. 'Harpoons? What the hell does a girl your age need with harpoons,' he said.

Rosie O'Donnell

Dad raised me to get outside, get muddy, and most of all – get on with it.

Sarah Ferguson, Duchess of York

Past experience indicates that the best way of dealing with my daughter is total attention and love.

Lyndon B. Johnson

It isn't that I'm a weak father, it's just that Jane's a strong daughter!

Henry Fonda

I live with a French woman and my four daughters. I live with
all these females and not one of them can cook. I'm so sick of
the female sensibility. I know they have to be on the phone
all the time but do they have to have all these lipsticks and
bottles everywhere? And the smells! Why can't women smell of
something that isn't a smell?

Bob Geldof

The father of a daughter is nothing but a high-class hostage.
A father turns a stony face to his sons, berates them, shakes
his antlers, paws the ground, snorts, runs them off into the
underbrush, but when his daughter puts her arm over his
shoulder and says, 'Daddy, I need to ask you something,' he is a
pat of butter in a hot frying pan.

Garrison Keillor

I know I have my father, Charlton, wrapped around my
little finger but he has us wrapped around his.

Holly Heston

My dear Anne, it would be in vain for me to try to send
you any news. I can only send you my love, and that is
anything but news. It is as old as you are.

Henry Wadsworth Longfellow

I didn't have the balls to vote against my father, Ronald Reagan, but I couldn't vote for him.

Patti Davis

Things not to worry about: don't worry about popular opinion; don't worry about dolls; don't worry about the past.

F. Scott Fitzgerald, letter to his daughter

I have three daughters and I find as a result I played King Lear almost without rehearsal.

Peter Ustinov

My older daughter has been living away from home for well over a decade now. She has a steady boyfriend and we get on just fine. But every so often, when I see them together, a strange urge comes over me to sit him down and ask him if his intentions are honourable.

Jon Carroll

Your son is your son till he takes a wife, but your daughter is your daughter for all of your life.

Spencer Tracy, **Father of the Bride**

Like Father, Like Son

FATHERS AND SONS

What are little boys made of?
What are little boys made of?
Frogs and snails,
And puppy-dogs' tails,
That's what boys are made of.

Nursery rhyme

Which are harder to raise, boys or girls? Has to be girls. Boys are easy. Give them a box of matches and they're happy.

Milton Berle

The fact that boys are allowed to exist at all is evidence of a remarkable Christian forbearance among men.

Ambrose Bierce

I have always thought that the initial trouble between me and my father was that he couldn't see the slightest purpose in my existence.

Laurence Olivier

Bobby, if you weren't my son, I'd hug you.

Hank Hill, **King of the Hill**

It was our son who kept our marriage together: neither of us wanted custody of him.

Chubby Brown

Boyhood is the natural state of rascality.

Herman Melville

I never got along with my dad. Kids would come up to me and say, 'My dad can beat up your dad.' And I'd say, 'Okay. When?'

Bill Hicks

I had dinner with my father last night, and made a classic Freudian slip. I meant to say, 'Please pass the salt,' but it came out, 'You prick, you ruined my childhood.'

Jonathan Katz

Lizzie Borden took an axe
And gave her mother forty whacks;
When she saw what she had done
She gave her father forty-one!

American rhyme

Father thought a day out huntin' taught you much more than a day at school.

Dick Francis

My father took me fishing once. He marched me to the riverbank and snapped a picture of me with a fishing rod in my hand, then we went home.

Andrei Codrescu

A man knows he is growing old because he begins to look like his father.

Gabriel García Márquez

I turned on the TV in a hotel room and there was a movie I was in. I watched for a while and thought, hey, I'm not a bad actor. Only later did I realize it was my son, Michael.

Kirk Douglas

There must always be a struggle between a father and son, while one aims at power and the other at independence.

Samuel Johnson

Life Lessons for Fathers

Shall I tell you something strange? Well, when I became a father I understood God.

Honoré de Balzac

At the birth of your child, you forgive your parents everything, without a second thought, like a velvet revolution. This is part of the cunning of babies.

Martin Amis

You must allow room for disagreement. I always encouraged Tiger to question what I was saying and, if he found me in error, to let me know so I could learn, too. In this way, parents can learn from their children.

Earl Woods

By the time a man realizes that maybe his father was right, he usually has a son who thinks he's wrong.

Charles Wadsworth

Older Fathers

I had my first son when I was 18. I was young and stupid and I grew up with the children. Having a son at 60, when I'm older and established, means that I can wallow in the parenthood thing.

Paul Hogan

Congratulations are in order for Woody Allen – he and Soon Yi have a brand new baby daughter. It's all part of Woody's plan to grow his own wives.

David Letterman

Catherine Zeta is the mother; I'm the official burper.

Michael Douglas

– What a man you are, maestro. You had children in your seventies!
– Yes, but I couldn't pick them up!

Interviewer and Pablo Picasso

Absent Fathers

– Jane. It's been a long time.
– Yes.
– How are the children?
– We didn't have any children.
– Yes, of course.

Lieutenant Frank Drebin and Jane Spencer, The Naked Gun 2½

My father died in childbirth.

Woody Allen

Like most fathers at that time, my father wasn't there, but, in a way, that can be a blessing. Familiarity breeds contempt.

Jack Ford

A man who does not spend time with his family can never be a real man.

Mario Puzo

Remembering Dad

It doesn't matter who my father was; it matters who I remember he was.

Anne Sexton

I remember watching TV with my dad; wrestling and jumping up and down with him in my room. We did a lot of drawing. He would scribble circles and squiggles on a piece of paper, and I would have to turn it into whatever I saw in them. With him, every day was an adventure. It was like my dad and I were buddies, and there was no real sorrow then.

Sean Lennon on John Lennon

I can't remember my father at all. I can remember my mother only through a child's eyes. I don't know which fact is the sadder.

Clive James

This is a moment that I deeply wish my parents could have lived to share. My father would have enjoyed what you have so generously said of me; and my mother would have believed it.

Lyndon B. Johnson, speech at Baylor University

My Heart Belongs to Daddy

LOVE

A child's spirit is like a child, you can never catch it by running after it; you must stand still, and, for love, it will soon itself come back.

Arthur Miller

It wasn't until my daughter was 2 years old and realized she was stuck with me that she said, during a walk through autumn leaves, 'I love you.'

James Thurber

Sorry, honey, I can't take you to the mall. Daddy loves you, but Daddy also loves Star Trek, and in all fairness, Star Trek was here first.

Peter Griffin, **Family Guy**

Unlike the male codfish, which suddenly finding itself the parent of 3,500,000 little codfish, cheerfully resolves to love them all, the British aristocracy is apt to look with a somewhat jaundiced eye on its younger sons.

P.G. Wodehouse

Index

Picture Credits

The publishers would like to thank the following sources for their kind permission to reproduce the pictures in this book:

ALL PHOTOGRAPHS SUPPLIED
BY CORBIS IMAGES

6:	A. Green/Zefa	82:	Rainer Holz/Zefa
10:	Sandra Seckinger/Zefa	86:	G. Baden/Zefa
14:	Larry Williams/Zefa	90:	Tom Stewart
18–19:	LWA-Sharie Kennedy/Zefa	94:	Creasource
22:	Benelux/Zefa	98:	Simon Marcus
26:	Jose Luis Pelaez, Inc.	102:	B. Bird/Zefa
30:	Left Lane Productions	106–107:	Tom Stewart
34:	Kim Eriksen/Zefa	110:	Bettina Schaefer/Zefa
38:	Larry Williams/Zefa	114:	Bob Thomas
42:	A. Green/Zefa	118:	Mark Seelen/Zefa
46–47:	Ronnie Kaufman/Zefa	122:	Simon Marcus
50–51:	Gary Salter/Zefa	126:	Ted Horowitz
54:	Gulliver/Zefa	134:	Grace/Zefa
58:	Gary Salter/Zefa	138:	Christian Weigel/Solus-Veer
62–63:	Randy Faris	142:	C. Devan/Zefa
66–67:	Ariel Skelley	146:	Tim Pannell
70–71:	Grace/Zefa	150:	Michael Prince
78:	Randy Faris	154–155:	Brigitte Sporrer/Zefa

Every effort has been made to acknowledge correctly and contact the source and/or copyright holder of each picture, and Carlton Books Limited apologises for any unintentional errors or omissions which will be corrected in future editions of this book.